What p

Lyn Smith ...

Lyn Smith writes with authority, clarity and conviction about the things that matter most. Her words challenge and inspire all of us to become more like Christ in how we think, speak and behave in our daily lives. You can be confident that Lyn's teachings will highlight the Truth, and if you let it, stir up the gifts of God that are within you.

Tommy Newberry
New York Times **best-selling author of** *The 4:8 Principle*

Lyn Smith is a gifted Bible teacher. Her love of God's Word and His people is evident in her daily life as she seeks to make disciples and help others grow in grace. She not only proclaims God's Word, but she models its application for those around her. Her Christ-like example and her godly wisdom are what led me to invite Lyn to serve on the Advisory Board for Living Bread Ministries.

Patrick Hubbard
Founder & President, *Living Bread Ministries*

What a privilege it is to know Lyn Smith and to benefit from her years of experience as a student of God's Word! She is as intentional as she is gifted - a Christ-honoring combination that makes her a trustworthy voice of truth for our generation.

Shelley Hendrix
Author, Founder of *Church 4 Chicks*, Co-Captain of *Team RedeeMEd*

The first time I met Lyn was during our speaking trip to Nigeria. Over the years, my respect for her as a Godly woman, loving wife, devoted mother, gifted speaker and shoe connoisseur has grown. Lyn consistently offers wisdom with a genuine empathy that few possess. Her writing will inspire you to grow deeper and serve stronger in Jesus' name.

Dr. J.R. Miller
Professor at *Southern California Seminary* and Teaching Elder for *Reunion Church*.

I can't think of a more important study than Psalm 119. Lyn Smith is one of my favorite Bible teachers and my first call for Bible questions. She lives Psalm 119. This study will strengthen your defense against the temptations of your heart and the ways of the world. Your love for God's Word will lead to more peace and confidence than you ever thought possible.

Jennifer O. White
Author of *Prayers for New Brides* (Spring, 2015) and Founder of *Prayerfully Speaking*

The power and passion in which Lyn Smith displays the love of our Lord in this God-inspired Psalm 119 workbook is simply breath-taking! As a Bible teacher, Lyn brings the knowledge of God in a way readers at any level in their spiritual growth can grasp and understand. As a member of *The Discipling Women: Damage Control* television show, Lyn shares nuggets of truth, empowering others with the Word of God. If you desire a clearer understanding of the power of God, we humbly suggest that you read and engage in the Psalm experience.

Shawn D. Savage, M.A.T.S. and Caroline R. Savage, D.M.
Savage Ministries International, Co-Founders of *Christian Discipleship Women's Ministry International*

Lyn Smith's Bible study on Psalm 119 not only challenged our lives, it renewed our hearts and reminded us that His Word is our source for victorious living. We were blessed to have Lyn lead our class. The participation and response to her godly wisdom was incredible. This same wisdom fills her Bible study. A wonderful study for a large or small group. Your women will love it and move closer to Christ.

Barbara Houston
Pastor of Women's Ministry, Crossings Community Church

Responses from WORD Participants

"Wow, if I didn't need this today! Wow! Glory! Amen!"

"After finishing the Psalm 119 study, I was left hungering for more ... more passion for God's Word and more love for God Himself!"

"Lyn's study of Psalm 119 has been life changing!

"Study rocked this morning! Seriously lovin' it."

"This has comforted and encouraged me for some hard challenges."

"Awesome Bible study! Thank you!"

"Insightful teaching."

"I have heard many Bible teachers through the years and NONE has been a better communicator of God's Word than Lyn Smith! I had the privilege of being involved in her Psalm 119 study. Lyn will make Psalm 119 everyone's favorite Psalm. There is no one I could recommend more than Lyn Smith."

"Blessings, praising, rejoicing, delighting! WOO HOO! This does my heart good!"

"Lyn, thanks for sharing your burning passion for God and His Word. I have enjoyed this study SO MUCH."

"Loved the study this morning, Lyn. You and Jesus rock!"

WORD

Psalm 119: A Study in 22 Meditations

Lyn Smith

Published by:

TRINITY WEB WORKS, LLC.
189 Liberty Street NE, Suite 210
Salem, Oregon, 97301 USA

Word
Copyright © 2014 by Lyn Smith

ISBN-13: 978-1533199256
ISBN-10: 1533199256

Library of Congress Catalog Card Number:

Printed in the United States of America

To the One Who knows me completely and loves me relentlessly ...

Thank You for fanning into flame a passion for You and Your Word that burns hotter the longer I live. I offer this simple book with gratitude that goes beyond words. Jesus, use it to make Your name and Your magnificence more widely known.

"Your name and renown are the desire of our hearts."
Isaiah 26:8b

CONTENTS

How To Experience WORD

I owe a *huge* thanks to the precious people who have experienced WORD in its various forms. I'm convinced there is an extra jewel in their heavenly crowns. Their feedback helped me land on the ways Psalm 119 can be most effectively experienced.

Suggestion #1: in a group, with videos

Small and large groups can benefit from this experience. An encouraged format is to meet together to discuss some of the book questions first, and then to watch the corresponding downloaded video. A facilitator can guide the discussion, having some of the questions answered in the large group and some discussed more intimately in small groups around tables.

You might prefer to break into small groups to handle the book questions exclusively that way, and then gather together for the videos.

Videos can be downloaded from www.lynsmith.org

The Experience Plan and Video Experiences are intended to be done in six weeks. However, you are welcome to tailor the experience to meet the needs of your group.

Suggestion #2: individually, with or without videos

Since my first walk through Psalm 119 took place between only me and God, I designed this experience to also work well as a personal tool for individuals.

You can watch the video downloads along with your Psalm 119 experience or simply enjoy your time with God, your Bible and the book.

The videos contain additional information, the expansion of concepts introduced in the book, and real life examples of how God's Word changes us.

If you choose to use them, the videos can be downloaded from www.lynsmith.org.

Experience Plan:

for <u>Session One</u> - no preparation, begin with Video #1

for <u>Session Two</u> - prepare the Introduction & Meditations 1-4

for <u>Session Three</u> - prepare Meditations 5-8

for <u>Session Four</u> - prepare Meditations 9-12

for <u>Session Five</u> - prepare Meditations 13-17

for <u>Session Six</u> - prepare Meditations 18-22 & Closing

***WORD* is most compatible with the New International Version®. Although other translations and paraphrases are quoted, the fill-in-the-blanks and questions will be most easily answered from the NIV.

***A Facebook community has been formed where you can share this experience with many others. Please join us at *The Psalm 119 Experience.*

Your Psalm 119

experience begins now ...

Video Experience One

The Bible is many things:

Primarily, the Bible is

_____.

Hesed is a Hebrew word for _____.

The unique meaning of *hesed* is

_____.

Three important points about the *hesed* of God:

1) It is _____ toward His children.

2) It is _____ toward His children.

3) It is _____ toward His children.

*** God's _____ _____ to us is worth

our utmost _____ and _____.

(videos are available for download at www.lynsmith.org)

Introduction

Why Psalm 119?

My childhood was golden … except for the ongoing sexual abuse, which I share more of in the videos. Setting that aside for now, however ...

God gave me godly parents who were committed to living out Christ in their lives and in our home. We read the Bible together as a family daily and often sang hymns around the piano. Yes, we were *that* family in the Norman Rockwell paintings.

One of my favorite songs as a child was "Holy Bible, Book Divine" written by John Burton, Sr. (1803).

> *"Holy Bible, book divine,*
> *Precious treasure, thou art mine.*
> *Mine to tell me whence I came.*
> *Mine to teach me Whose I am."*

Those words still resonate deeply within me. In fact, the truth and power of those words kept me sane during my years of abuse and destructive behaviors. They still do! I read God's words every day, memorize them, hold them dearly in my heart, and use them to live the astounding life God gives me daily. They have power that I need and draw upon with every breath.

I used to teach an in-depth Bible class every year from September through May. Eight years ago I went through a difficult spring and began to wonder how I would survive the summer without that Bible study. As I began to pray about what I should read during those months to stay close to God, He directed my thoughts toward Psalm 119. Even though it is the longest chapter in the Bible with 176 verses, it didn't seem possible that it would keep me interested the entire summer. I continued to pray over it, expressing my skepticism to God, but He kept saying, "Live in Psalm 119. All summer."

I am so glad I listened to God and followed his promptings. Immersing myself in Psalm 119 changed my life. The emphasis of the Psalm is the Word of God. I thought I knew His Word but the treasures in those 176 verses were richer, deeper, and more satisfying than I could have imagined. In three months, I barely skimmed the surface of all God placed in that Psalm. Each phrase, each verse, and each section exploded into my heart, mind, and life as I walked out the truths God was revealing. In the years since as I have taught Psalm 119 to groups and gone deeper into it myself, I have found it to be bottomless. Every time I study it, God shows me more of Himself and gives me more life application.

His words are precious, powerful and fail proof! As you meditate on and live out the verses of Psalm 119, you will develop unshakable confidence in Him and a sweeter intimacy with Him than you have ever known.

I encourage you to make personal notes in your Bible as you go through this book. Make Psalm 119 *your* Psalm. Document this journey so it becomes a reference point of who God is in your life and what He does. Highlight significant phrases and record your thoughts in the margins. Your personal study Bible is not meant to be beautifully displayed on a coffee table. Use it!

This first section has more reading than the others but I want you to enjoy the beautiful perspective from which this Psalm was likely written.

What is Psalm 119?

Psalm 119 is a repetitive meditation on the benefits and power of God's Word. It is divided into twenty-two sections of eight verses each. Each section corresponds to a different letter in the Hebrew alphabet, and each verse begins with the letter of its section. Almost every verse mentions God's Word. Such repetition was common in the Hebrew culture. People didn't have personal copies of the Scriptures to read as we do, so God's people memorized His Word and passed it along orally. The structure of this Psalm allowed for easy memorization.[1]

Unless you are reading along in a Hebrew Bible you won't get the full impact of how beautifully this Psalm flows. However, in any language the simple strength of these verses will be obvious and easy to grasp. Putting it into action and having it take root deep down in the soil of your heart for a lifetime will take more commitment, which is my prayer for you. This book isn't intended to be an easy read, but an experience of intimate force that propels you into a relentless pursuit of God.

I urge you to test and try in real life what you discover. My desire for you, and more importantly God's desire for you, is that you know beyond any doubt that God and His Word never fail. They are consistent, true, and backed by the perfect character of God Himself. They will never fail you. They will never fail the people you love. Bring every problem, concern, fear, desire, and need to the pages containing the very breath of God and you will be astounded at the results.

A surface reading of Scripture is never a waste of time but let's maximize our walk through Psalm 119 by understanding the context in which it was written. Even if you don't enjoy the study of history, you'll enjoy the story around this Psalm. Knowing who probably wrote it, why he wrote it, and the impact it had on the Hebrew people will open your mind to vast possibilities for your own personal growth. Travel back with me to around 450 B.C.

Some scholars believe Ezra could have written Psalm 119 after the temple was rebuilt. After spending seventy years in captivity in Babylon, Cyrus, King of Persia, allowed the Hebrew people to return to their land in order to build a temple for God in Jerusalem. Nearly 50,000 people returned in that first group, including the priests and Levites, whose job it was to minister in the temple and lead the people spiritually. Upon arriving in their homeland, the people contributed freely to the rebuilding of God's house, each giving according to his or her ability. Despite twenty-two years of planning, hard labor, opposition, discouragement and fear, the temple was completed.

"Then the people of Israel – the priests, the Levites and the rest of the exiles – celebrated the dedication of the house of God with joy." Ezra 6:16

Nearly sixty years later, Ezra, a descendant of Aaron the priest and *"a teacher well versed in the law of Moses"* (Ezra 7:6), arrived in Jerusalem with the second group of returning exiles. Upon arriving, however, he discovered that God's people, including the priests and Levites, had intermarried with neighboring pagans, adopting their detestable practices. Sadly, the leaders and officials had led the way in this unfaithfulness. God's leaders were full of sin! As the leaders go, so go the people.

Ezra grieved over the sin of God's people. He knew what they needed in order to return to their God – huge doses of His Word! Ezra knew what Paul so perfectly described hundreds of years later.

"All Scripture is God-breathed and is useful for teaching, rebuking, correcting and training in righteousness." 2 Timothy 3:16

Just as God breathed life into Adam, making people different from any other part of creation, God breathed His life into the Bible, making it different from any other book. When we pick up a Bible we are holding an organic book. It's alive! It has been infused with the very breath of God Almighty which never loses relevance or power. When we read it, the Bible speaks truth into our lives that changes us through the power of the Holy Spirit. His presence in us resonates spiritually with the words on the pages, creating a living dynamic that transforms our being. Ezra knew that to be true, even before God explained it through the writers of the New Testament. He had experienced it in his own life and had likely seen it lived in the lives of others.

All the people assembled, and Ezra began to read aloud from the Law. At the first reading, he read from daybreak until noon, while all the people listened attentively. When he opened the book, the people all stood up. The Levites helped instruct the people while they were standing there. *"They read from the book of the Law of God, making it clear and giving the meaning so that the people could understand what was being read."* (Nehemiah 8:8) In response to hearing the words of God, revival broke out among the people! Great weeping and confession was followed by great joy and celebration.

"They stood where they were and read from the Book of the Law of the Lord their God for a quarter of a day, and spent another quarter in confession and in worshiping the Lord their God." Nehemiah 9:3

The people made a new covenant with God to separate from their sin and faithfully live for Him. Only the words of God and the conviction of the Holy Spirit can change lives so dramatically. I have experienced this supernatural phenomenon in my own life and want it for you too.

In the context of that story, it won't surprise me at all to discover when I get to heaven that Ezra did write Psalm 119. The power and beauty of God's Word washing over the people brought about a nationwide revival. Revival is a restoration to life, consciousness, vigor, and strength.[2]

Imagine what had happened in each heart to result in such a public and widespread response! Can you picture Ezra writing Psalm 119 in praise of God's Word after experiencing that revival? Or maybe he wrote it to prompt the revival by reminding them of the power of God's Word. Either way, its power and beauty still cleanse and fill our hearts today.

Does the story of the Hebrew revival cause you to long for a fresh reviving of your own heart?

Maybe you are simply wondering if the Bible has anything to offer you. Or you may be approaching this experience with skepticism, and that is okay.

No matter where you are in life: your age, your past, your concerns, your questions, your circumstances, or your years of Bible study, I invite you to walk with me through Psalm 119. If you honestly seek God, I guarantee that not only will He be found but He will astound you!

"'You will seek me and find me when you seek me with all your heart. I will be found by you,' declares the Lord ..." Jeremiah 29:13-14a

"Call to me and I will answer you. I'll tell you marvelous and wondrous things that you could never figure out on your own." Jeremiah 33:3 (The Message)

Where do you need a fresh infusion of God's power?

Where do you need cleansing or inspiration?

Where do you need courage to be obedient?

Do you want a transformed mind?

Do you desire to fall in love with Jesus, for the first time or in a deeper way?

On a scale from 1 (the least) to 10 (the most), how hungry are you for God? (circle a number)

1 2 3 4 5 6 7 8 9 10

Take a moment and ask God to give you a fresh longing for Him.
Now thank Him in advance for what He is going to do in you.

Meditation 1: Read Psalm 119:1-8

Life Lesson - Those whose whole-hearted walk with God is blameless, are blessed by Him.

Look back at vv. 1-2. Twice the writer says we are blessed. The literal meaning here of the word blessed is happy. Happy? We have all heard that God never promises we will be happy. Joyful, yes. Happy, no. Happy, we are told, is frivolous and circumstantial. What we are promised and what we should desire is deep, abiding joy regardless of circumstances. However, right here in black and white we are told that Christians are blessed. We can be happy! In fact, God promises it.

Before you close your Bible and head into your day, claiming God's promise of happiness, take a look at a few more phrases. Understanding specific verses in the context of their paragraph or chapter is often crucial: it truly is here.

This Psalm is about God's Word. The Psalmist uses different words to refer to it: law(s), statutes, ways, precepts, decrees, commands, word, and promise. We will discover, as we go along, that the key to understanding the nuances of this Psalm is the whole of God's Word. We will look into chapters other than Psalm 119 to clarify and expand various truths.

Yes, God wants us to be happy, but how? By meeting four conditions.

❖ What are they? (vv. 1-2)

The word 'walk' in v. 1 conveys the idea of a continuous action. We keep walking. As we walk every day with God, we will obey what we read in His Word. This simple process is designed to be done consistently. We set out on the path of belonging to God and knowing God. We are to stay on that path all the time. If you are like me, your first reaction is to say, "How? With the busyness of life and the distractions of the world, how can I walk with God all the time?" Such a practical and honest question receives a practical and honest answer in v. 2 – seek Him with all your heart.

❖ Describe what it means to you to seek God with all your heart.

It sounds as though God is asking for perfection from us in vv. 3-4, but He is not. He is asking for a heart that loves and seeks Him above all else. He does not just want part of you. He wants *all* of you. When you allow Him to flood your heart and mind with Himself and His Word, when you hold back nothing from Him, you will know true happiness.

❖ What is the honest cry of the Psalmist's heart in v. 5?

❖ Is that your cry, too?

We long to obey but often find ourselves doing just the opposite. Do not despair! God is more interested in our hearts than our behaviors because He knows that the condition of our hearts determines our behaviors. Be honest with Him and talk with Him through your disappointments with yourself. Let Him bathe you in His forgiveness and love.

What does God promise when we know His Word? v. 6

❖ What two "I will" commitments result from seeking God with our whole heart? vv. 7-8

The more we know of God, the more we are filled with praise. Praise becomes a habitual response of our spirit and soul to His magnificence. We *will* praise Him when we succeed and we *will* praise Him when we fail. Praising Him for who He is, not for our circumstances, allows us to praise Him no matter what!

You know what you will discover? Praising God makes you happy.

❖ Describe your walk with God.

❖ What will you do to deepen your walk in the areas of seeking and obeying Him?

Write the Life Lesson from Meditation 1 in your own words:

Meditation 2: Read Psalm 119:9-16

Life Lesson - Memorizing and meditating on God's Word lead to victorious, joyful living.

Life is full of temptations! Some from without, some from within.

❖ List some temptations that come at you from your environment.

❖ List some that come from within your own heart and mind.

The Psalmist asks a perfect question for us, living in the twenty-first century. How in the world can a young person, or any person for that matter, remain pure? With suggestions all around us to engage in destructive behavior, how can we sift out what is right from what is wrong?

What is considered acceptable changes practically every day. Is there a standard that is right for everyone? Is there a way to remain morally pure in our morally bankrupt culture? Yes!! Yes!! Yes!! If we live according to God's Word, if we raise up His standard of holiness in our lives, we can walk the blameless life referred to in vv. 1-2.

Just reading it, though, is not enough. We have to sink our teeth into it, digest it, and let it nourish our souls. God's words have to take root deep in our hearts in order to be effective when temptation comes. Part of that process is the daily reading that washes over us and steadily transforms our thinking.

❖ What is the other part? v. 11

Jesus did it. That was how He defeated Satan's temptations in the wilderness.

❖ How many times did Jesus quote Scripture in Matthew 4:1-11?

❖ Ephesians 6:10-18 describes the pieces of our spiritual armor. Which two pieces are truth and God's Word?

❖ What exciting things begin to happen when we meditate on God's Word and experience victory over sin? Psalm 119: 13-16

That description should be true of every follower of Jesus Christ. *That* is the abundant life described throughout the New Testament. I so want that for you!

You know where you tend to sin. Use a concordance or online resource to write on note cards or sticky notes several verses that address your areas of temptation and sin. Carry those with you for weeks until the verses immediately spring to mind when temptation comes. Say them over and over until the temptation passes. Another suggestion is to place your cards in a clear plastic bag and hang it in the shower. There is no better thing to do with your mind in the shower than memorize Scripture! That is hiding God's Word in your heart that you might not sin (v. 11).

Write the Life Lesson from Meditation 2 in your own words:

Meditation 3: Read Psalm 119:17-24

Life Lesson – Having my heart and mind full of God's Word enables me to handle difficult relationships.

How nice it would be if a blameless walk and a whole heart for God resulted in easy, pleasant relationships. Unfortunately, we live in a world of fallen people who are sometimes insensitive, selfish, pushy, mean spirited, and critical. Christ followers are not exempt from those behaviors either. Especially when we are tired or sick we easily revert back to old attitudes, causing tension or hurt feelings.

After beautifully encouraging us to walk wholeheartedly with God, the Psalmist now brings up a challenging area – other relationships. However, he first wisely reminds us of some crucial truths that help us in our relationships.

❖ Verse 17 reminds us of God's sustaining power. It is God who is good to us. It is God who sustains our life. Look up and write the definition of "sustain."

❖ Explain in your own words how God sustains you.

There is an important cause and effect here. When we understand how good God is to us, and how dependent we are on His sustaining power, we are eager and willing to obey.

❖ As we read God's Word, for what should we ask? v. 18

Verse 19 tells us why we should ask. We are strangers here –
different from those around us. We need God's wisdom to live
the victorious life He has for us.

❖ As we journey with God, with what should our souls be
   consumed? v. 20

❖ Is that true of you?

When we seek Him with all our hearts, God fills us with
Himself in a way that relieves the desperate longings we might
have for something or someone else. The earthly benefits we
enjoy are just icing on the cake compared to the depth of
intimacy we receive with Him. Loving my spouse and children
is like nibbling on the cherry perched atop a hot fudge sundae.
It is sweet and delicious! But I know that the real satisfaction
will come as I delve into the ice cream and hot fudge below.
With that foundation in place, we can begin applying God's
Word to our earthly relationships.

Take a moment to ask God to open your eyes to see the
wonderful things He wants to teach you about relationships.

❖ Carefully read vv. 21-24 and list the words that describe
   these challenging people.

You may have not experienced all of them but because you live
on this planet, you have experienced at least one. Arrogant
people who stray from God's commands act on their own
prideful thinking. They believe they are right and expect others
to bend to their ways. They often have little tolerance for
anything or anyone they consider beneath them. Their
condescending attitude can be extremely harsh and hurtful.
There are those who mock us for our faith, the way we look,
our education, or where we live. Others may gossip about us,

or purposefully attempt to turn friends against us. Whoever said that sticks and stones may break our bones but words will never hurt us, had never been verbally slashed to ribbons by someone they trusted. Our first response to criticism and slander should be to go to God's Word. His Word is our delight! It counsels us wisely every time. It gives us examples of how to respond to hurtful or difficult people. The Bible reminds us that God is our defender so we don't have to defend ourselves. God's holy, authoritative, perfect Word addresses every need and problem we have, including relational challenges.

Jesus is the ultimate example of how to respond to the worst of abuse. Many times He was silent, allowing His Father to handle His abusers. Other times He spoke truth that challenged the thoughts and intentions of the abuser. The words He spoke were *always* intended to enlighten and help the other person. He never spoke harshly out of selfishness or a desire to hurt. If you are suffering at the mouth of a verbal abuser, carefully read Matthew 26-28 and make note of Jesus' responses to a variety of people and situations. God will give you that same wisdom in your responses.

❖ How do you usually respond to harsh words?

❖ How does God want you to respond to harsh words? (Psalm 17:3, Psalm 19:14, Proverbs 15:1, Galatians 5:22, Ephesians 4:29, James 1:19)

❖ Do you need to ask forgiveness from someone with whom you have been harsh?

❖ Where do you go for counsel when facing a relational problem?

❖ According to v. 24, where should you go first, and with what attitude?

Write the Life Lesson from Meditation 3 in your own words.

Meditation 4: Read Psalm 119:25-32

Life Lesson – Living God's Word is the path of freedom.

❖ What three painful situations do you see in vv. 25, 28, and 29?

Life is full of difficulties! Jesus promised it would be, so we know not to be surprised by them. Because God knows it too, He gave us His Word to help us navigate through the mine fields. If you sense you are about to step on a mine or if you just did, take heart, my friend. There is a path through the mine fields of life that leads to glorious freedom.

We see two patterns emerging in this section that continue throughout the Psalm.

Pattern #1: "God preserves my life." (v. 25)
The Psalmist uses that phrase nine times, which means we need to sit up and take notice. We will see that God preserves our lives by several means, this first one being His Word. Other translations use quicken (KJV) and revive (Amplified) instead of preserve. The original word in Hebrew literally means to keep alive. It also has the component of nourishing, restoring and recovering.[3] Not only does God's Word keep us alive but it also feeds and heals us along the way.

How can a book keep us alive?

1) Only *this* book has the power to sustain life because it is infused with God's power.

❖ According to 2 Timothy 3:16, all Scripture is what?

❖ How does Hebrews 4:12 describe the Bible?

2) It keeps us alive by giving wisdom and hope. Psalm 119: 27 enlarges those truths.

As we read the Bible we are to ask God for help in understanding His teaching. He promises to give wisdom to those who ask and does so through the illuminating power of the Holy Spirit within. As we gain wisdom, we begin making better decisions. We have new eyes that see clear ways of handling difficult situations that were previously cloudy. We also begin to see the dangers in those deceitful ways ahead of time instead of falling into the potholes.

❖ According to Isaiah 48:17, what does God do for us?

Wisdom is a sweet companion!

Looking again at Psalm 119:27 we see how wisdom flows into hope. When we understand God's Word, when our view of God gets bigger, then we can meditate on His wonders. As I meditate on His wonders revealed in His Word, awe fills my soul. I marvel at His majesty, splendor and mighty power. His love embraces me and I am caught up in the glory of belonging to Him. How can I *not* have hope? He is my All in All! He is the One and Only! He is the Bright Morning Star that floods my days with light. Surrounded by Him and filled with passion for Him, knowing He has me in the palm of His hand, there is no room for despair. Fear flees!

3) It keeps us alive by giving strength. Psalm 119:28

❖ How are we, who read and meditate on Scripture, described in Psalm 1:2-3?

❖ How does Jesus describe us in Matthew 7:24-25?

I am alive and can do all things through Christ who gives me strength!

Pattern #2: "path" (v. 32)
"Path" is used throughout the Psalm six times. It is used in several ways but in verse 32, it is used as the path of God's commands. We deliberately choose this path as our road of life, which is completely opposite from the road of deceitful ways.

What is the four-fold progression in vv. 30-32? (NIV)

I have _____ (v. 30)

I have _____ (v. 30)

I _____ _____ (v. 31)

I _____ (v. 32)

We choose God's ways and set our hearts on His laws. Then we earnestly hold fast to them as we do what? *Run* in the path of freedom. Liberating, joyous, exuberant, life-changing freedom. Freedom comes through our obedience to God's Word that we have chosen, set our hearts on and held fast to.

If you are experiencing one or all of the scenarios mentioned at the beginning of this meditation, you need not be in bondage to them. As difficult as they may be, you are not without answers. You are not without hope. Soak your mind in God's Word, talk to Him about your life (v. 26), and live out obedience in your situations. Then run like the wind along the path of freedom!

❖ What difficulty are you facing or in the middle of today?

❖ How will you rely on God's Word to preserve you through it?

❖ What obedience will it require? Are you willing to trust God with the outcome?

❖ Will you choose God's way today instead of your own or someone else's?

❖ Will you set your heart on God's Word today and hold fast to it?

If you honestly answered yes to those two questions, put on your running shoes, hit the path, and enjoy a heart set free!

Write the Life Lesson from Meditation 4 in your own words.

Video Experience Two

<u>Exploring three words</u>

1) _____

Christian _____ :

2) _____

    a. _____ _____

b. _____ _____ _____

3) _____

*** _____, _____, and

_____ begin with Jesus Christ and

_____ _____ with the study of

God's Word.

(videos are available for download at www.lynsmith.org)

Meditation 5: Read Psalm 119:33-40

Life Lesson - Praying for and seeking the things of God keep me from worthless things that waste my life.

Do you ever get to the end of a day and wonder where it went? We look back over those sixteen or so hours and know we were busy. Our exhausted minds and bodies tell us that. But what did we actually accomplish that has any real value?

Read 1 Corinthians 3:11-15

When our activities go through the testing fire, as we are told they will, will they all burn up as useless? Are we building piles of wood, hay and stubble? Did we impact anyone with the love of Christ? God gave us this day for a reason. Are we fulfilling that reason?

This section of Psalm 119 gives us six ways to pray at the beginning of each new day: (NIV)

1) _____ ____, O Lord, ____ _____ your decrees. v. 33

Jesus commanded His disciples to follow Him. The command is no less important for us today. We are to walk in His footprints all day long. Jesus is not tricky or confusing or condescending. He is not out to frustrate us by leaving vague footprints or by taking such big steps that we cannot possibly reach them. Oh no, friends. Our Lord Jesus is our biggest fan, our greatest cheerleader, and our very best friend. He wants our success more than we do! He lays out His plans for us in His Word, so our obvious first step in a purposeful day is to read it and ask Him to teach us to follow it.

Bible = Basic Instructions Before Leaving Earth

2) _____ me _____. v. 34

When our intent is obedience, God will give us understanding of His Word and will. He never mocks His children! He gave us His Holy Spirit to enable us to grasp spiritual, eternal truths. When we read our Bibles and sincerely ask for understanding, the Holy Spirit gives us what we need. Some especially deep or complex things need to simmer awhile as our minds and hearts meditate on them. Place those things on the back burner and trust the Holy Spirit to do His gentle work of illuminating truth over time.

3) _____ me. v. 35

God's primary way of directing us is in His Word. As we consistently read and pray over it, He gives direction. If you are looking for a verse with your name in it specifically telling you to buy that item, you won't find it. God's Word directs us through truthful statements, examples, universal principles, commands, and promises. As we read and live those things, a marvelous spiritual activity takes place. The Holy Spirit of God Himself impresses His direction upon our minds and hearts.

❖ How does Isaiah 30:21 describe His activity?

4) _____ my _____. v. 36

We are to turn our hearts toward the truth of God, what brings honor and glory to Him, not toward things and activities that promote ourselves. Pray for a love of the things that promote *God*!

❖ How does Philippians 4:8 describe those things to which we turn our hearts?

Evaluate your activities according to that description and you will quickly see the ones that are for selfish gain. Turning requires action, so as God works in your heart, expect change.

5) _____ my _____ v. 37

Hebrews 12:2 tells us to fix our eyes on Jesus. Our turning toward the truth of God and away from worthless things should ultimately result in a single focus. As His beauty and radiance fill our view, the things of this earthly life will grow dim compared to the light of His glory and grace. We will begin exchanging the tinsel of this world for the gold of heaven.

6) _____ Your _____. v. 38

The Amplified Bible says, "*Establish Your word and confirm Your promise.*" The combination of those thoughts teaches us that as God's Word takes root deeply in our hearts and becomes the foundation of our character, He fulfills His promise to complete His work in us (Philippians 1:6). What a relief! Our growth is His job. As you pray these six things, you can count on God to grow you and change you in ways that will astound you.

I have done more than my fair share of pursuing worthless things. Oh, the many had-to-have items that have broken, been given away, worn out or been thrown out! How much time, money and energy have been wasted on those things? Nothing seems to make that as clear as going through someone else's things - one who has passed on from this life. Certainly there are valuable and sentimental treasures, many that I cherish. But what about the cabinets full of seldom-used cookware, roll upon roll of wrapping paper, old magazines, half-empty paint cans, tools for which there is no longer a use, and stained potholders? Writing that list fills me with the urge to rid my life of worthless things. How about you? God has so much more for us than cabinets full of stuff! Let us long for His precepts and make room in our lives to study them.

If you have not already, take a few minutes to pray these six things. You may want to write the six statements and place them somewhere as a reminder to pray them every day.

❖ What worthless things in your life has God shown you during this section?

❖ Will you commit to a process of removing them?

❖ Will you trust God to replace them with delight in Him and His ways?

Ask God for a longing for Him and His Word above all else.

Write the Life Lesson from Meditation 5 in your own words.

Meditation 6: Read Psalm 119:41-48

Life Lesson - The more I read God's Word, the more I will love it and speak it.

God says many things about the tongue. A glance through Proverbs or a reading of James reveals some of His thoughts. Included are strong cautions and warnings of the tongue's destructive potential. We are given instructions on how to control it and commands to use it in certain ways. Proverbs, which often makes me laugh, points out the cause and effect of spoken words. This one is priceless, "*If a man loudly blesses his neighbor early in the morning, it will be taken as a curse*" (Proverbs 27:14). Being one who wakes up alert and ready to socialize, I have experienced that one firsthand!

What we see in this portion of Psalm 119 is somewhat different. The Psalmist describes the spontaneous outpouring of God's Word from the lips of one who is loving and living it. As we walk the path of reading the Bible and applying it to life, we experience more and more of God's love.

❖ What word describes God's love? v. 41

His love is always there but it is a process for us to learn to be aware of it, to trust it, and sometimes to actually feel it. As His love becomes the bedrock of our soul it begins to work its way out of us in daily situations through our words.

Three specific situations involving words are given:

1) Hostile people. v. 42

We can answer the one who taunts us with words of truth. Just as Jesus responded with Scripture, so can we. It is true, and works every time! And when it is fresh on our minds from our daily reading, it bubbles forth with sincerity, strength, and purpose. Our words become those that challenge, comfort, correct, encourage, subdue, build up, and penetrate. They become God's words, not our own, and we marvel at what just came out of our mouths. We find ourselves blessing instead of cursing.

"To bless" someone literally means to wish someone well, to desire God's favor and blessing upon their lives.[4]

2) Daily life. v. 43

We can pray that the word of truth will always be in our mouths. It will always be our first response. God's Word will be a natural part of conversation. As a wise person said, with our words we contribute to others' lives rather than contaminate them. If we are constantly memorizing God's Word, reading it and studying it, then it will be the thing we want to talk about.

3) Before authorities. v. 46

We may get opportunities to speak His words before civil authorities, and because we trust His words, we will speak them without shame. Knowing, with that deep-in-the-soul certainty, that what we are saying is right and true emboldens us to speak it … no matter in whose presence we are. When we're trying to dodge or come up with something or stall, it is obvious. We stammer, turn red, and repeat ourselves. *But,* when we know the truth, have tested it, lived it, and loved it, we can speak it!

When we delight in His commands, when we love them with all our hearts, and when we meditate on them throughout the day, and even during the night, we change.

The Psalmist points out three welcomed changes:

1) I always _____. v. 44

This does not mean we are successful at it 100% of the time, but that it is the deep desire of our hearts to be so. Disobedience brings sorrow and repentance. Obedience brings joy, satisfaction, and peace.

2) I _____ about in _____. v. 45

We are not worrying over every little thing. Should I say this or that? Did that person ignore me? Do I look okay? We are free to trust God's truth and power within us to govern our thoughts and actions. We know the Holy Spirit will check us if we have overlooked someone or something important.

3) I _____ _____ my _____. v. 48

We praise God's Word, which we love. There is a new freedom of expression in worship, whether we are alone with God or worshiping corporately.

❖ What are some positions of prayer? Mark 11:25, Ephesians 3:14, Deuteronomy 9:25

❖ Which one(s) do you use? Do you have the freedom alone with God to use all of them?

❖ If not, why not?

In corporate settings, some people who want to worship freely get concerned about being distracting or inappropriate. While sensitivity to others is a God-honoring quality, if it is motivated by the Spirit it will never prioritize what people think over what God says. If the Spirit inside you is prompting you to worship, you don't need to be concerned about those around you. God will give them the grace to respond to the worship they see. He may even use one person's freedom in worship to release someone else's.

We don't go to church to be on display for one another. We go out of love for God and in order to build His kingdom.

❖ Can you find any situations in the Bible where God rebuked a person for authentic, public worship of Him?

The point is, when Jesus becomes a living, breathing part of our lives … when He truly is the One we wake up thinking about, longing to talk with, and eager to serve … when it is a real relationship not just a fact or an eternal destiny … our passion for Him and the way it is expressed becomes natural and unselfconscious.

You probably know the feeling of being head over heels in love. Everything about the person you love is fascinating. The three years before my husband and I married, we were at college together. He was (still is!) tall, handsome, broad shouldered, intelligent and extremely witty. You can imagine how enthralled I was and how I gushed about him to everyone who would listen. I could not NOT talk about him.

I have noticed the same glassy-eyed devotion in grandparents. I have no doubt their *children* are outstanding human beings but you rarely hear it listening to them talk about their *grandchildren*. In fact, sometimes it seems they skipped having children and went straight to grandchildren, such is their consuming love for them! I have yet to meet a grandparent who does not have pictures of their grandchildren, which they eagerly pull out and share stories about. Their delight and captivation is contagious.

❖ What do you most want to talk about? What consumes your conversations?

❖ What effect do you think your words and expressions have on other people? Would you be courageous enough to ask several family members or trusted friends? Be sure to explain why you are asking and give them the freedom to respond honestly.

❖ How confident are you in your responses to people? Do you worry over saying the "right thing?"

❖ Are you developing a love for God's Word? If yes, how can you tell?

❖ Are you beginning to experience more freedom in your words and expressions?

Ask God to continue that work in you and trust Him to do it!

May I offer a few words of encouragement? If your true desire is to have a mouth filled with praise and appropriate words, yet you struggle with the habit of crude words, God knows your heart is toward obedience. Keep on loving Him. Keep on seeking Him in His Word. Keep asking Him to wash your mind of those dishonoring words and fill it and your mouth with His perfect words. He will do it, but remember it is a process.

Hang in there. He is so proud of you!

Write the Life Lesson from Meditation 6 in your own words.

Meditation 7: Read Psalm 119:49-56

Life Lesson - God's Word comforts and strengthens me as I read and obey it.

Have you felt overwhelmed recently? Has life thrown a curveball that knocked you off balance? Perhaps it is worse than that and you are in the depths of a pit…darkness threatening to enclose you…a sense of impending doom… Hold on! God is greater than your despair.

❖   What does verse 49 tell us God gives us?

Hidden in that verse is a simple but powerful formula that can revolutionize our thinking and responses.

God + His Word = HOPE

That formula is the divine lifeline, the flotation device needed to keep our heads above water. We can cling to God and His Word as if our lives depend on them. As a matter of fact, they do! If we focus too much on the world around us, it will sink us. How can we not give in to utter despair when we are bombarded with images of war, disease, malnutrition, poverty, natural disasters and death?

Bringing it closer to home for some … staggering debt, loss of a job, cancer, Alzheimer's, Parkinson's, a special needs child, no medical coverage, failed career goal, dying parent, child struggling in destructive sin, our own sin that holds us captive, a broken engagement, cold marriage, heartbreaking divorce. I feel the weight of despair just writing those words. But we have to acknowledge the bad news before we can truly embrace the good news.

❖ What is our comfort in suffering? v. 50

God's promises motivate us in the good times and sustain us in the hard times. Unlike human beings, God never breaks His promises. Once we get that hard wired into our minds, we can grab our Bibles when desperation strikes and begin praying and claiming God's promises. He will never leave us or forsake us! His presence and power are constant. He is always on our side, always fighting for us, always interceding for us, and always bigger than anything we face.

❖ What are three of your favorite promises from God?

❖ What word is used to describe God's laws? v. 52

The Hebrew word translated ancient (NIV) or old (KJV), means eternal and without end.[5]

God's words are timeless. That means they are true at all times, for all time. They exist as truth outside of time. Time does not diminish or change His truth.

God's words are eternal. Eternal in terms of time, and unlimited in depth. God's words contain so much truth and so much power that we cannot exhaust them. We will never plumb the depths of the Bible. Every time we open it, living words jump off the page giving us fresh inspiration or insight.

❖ How does Isaiah 55:9 describe that concept?

❖ The Psalmist says that is comforting to him. How is that comforting to you?

When we feel all hope is lost, God reminds us we stopped short. He has more for us. He IS more for us than we realized.

Not only are we comforted by God's promises but we find strength in them.

❖ What three scenarios are given where the Psalmist was helped by God's Word?

   Verse 51 –

   Verse 53 -

   Verse 54 –

❖ There is nowhere we can go from His presence. What are your thoughts after reading Psalm 139:7-10?

❖ According to Psalm 119:55, when did the writer think about God?

That time is often when strong temptations come, both in thought and action. Reviewing memorized verses, claiming God's promises, or going through the alphabet and naming an attribute of God for each letter are ways to protect ourselves and keep our minds pure.

❖ What is the Psalmist's stated practice (behavior)? v. 56

Today we might say, "This is who I am and what I do." I am a follower of Jesus Christ and I obey Him.

❖ To what or whom do you typically turn for help?

❖ In what situation do you currently need help?

❖ How do you usually seek comfort?

❖ Will you choose to go to His Word for comfort? Will you receive His promises as your own?

❖ Will you give your situation and responses to God today? Will you ask Him to show you His way?

❖ Will you commit right now to obey in whatever way He leads?

Write the Life Lesson from Meditation 7 in your own words.

Meditation 8: Read Psalm 119:57-64

Life Lesson - Walking close to God means lining up my life with His Word every day.

One of the great comforts of God's Word, and of God Himself, is consistency.

Consistent = constantly adhering to the same principles, course, and form.

Not only does the Bible tell the one amazing story of redemption all the way through, but its sub themes remain consistent to that story and to one another. An exciting thing we discover because of that is we can go to different places in the Bible for clarification or expansion of a truth. It is rather like a treasure hunt. We find intriguing clues along the way that keep us moving forward, anticipating a wonderful treasure ahead. I have expanded my knowledge and love of God using that process. A certain verse will raise a question in my mind that needs further information. I look in the margins or at the footnotes for verses that continue that topic, look them up, and keep going. Sometimes I use a concordance or Bible dictionary for help in pursuing an idea. I often end up spending my entire study time researching an idea that was not part of my plan at all. And, oh, the fun and joy I have in that deeper discovery that ultimately leads to deeper intimacy with my Lord!

Read verse 59 again. We are going to use it to begin a treasure hunt of this section.

❖ What does considering my ways involve? Is it mere introspection? Is it self-evaluation? How would you describe it?

Clue #1 – Read Psalm 139:23-24. What do you learn about considering your ways, and who else needs to be included?

Clue #2 – Read Amos 7:7-8. What earthly item does Amos use as an illustration of how God evaluates us?

Builders use these items to check the integrity of a wall. The string hangs straight down, revealing any crookedness of the wall.

❖ What was God's verdict when He measured Israel?

Our plumb line of holiness is God's Word. It is the standard by which we check our spiritual integrity. We listen to Him by turning our steps to the truths there. Considering my ways means holding the straight line of God's Word up against my thoughts, motives, words, and actions. Then I will be able to see any tilting or unevenness. I can identify the problem areas that are weakening my structure. A weak structure promises big problems ahead, so a wise builder deals with the crookedness as soon as he discovers it. To do that, let's take the final turn on our hunt and go back to our section of Psalm 119.

Clue #3 - There are six wise actions included here that when taken enable us to walk closely in line with God's standard of holiness.

God becomes my _____. v. 57
We make God our source of satisfaction. He becomes our joy, our peace and our fulfillment.

I seek Him with _____ _____ _____. v. 58

We are asked for 100% and nothing less. No other gods before Him. No idols of possessions, power, appearance or lust.

I commit to _____ His commands. v. 60
Obedience is to be immediate. Even if the action cannot be taken yet, the heart has said "yes" to God and begins the process of fulfilling the command.

I use the night hours to _____ Him _____. v. 62

I surround myself with godly _____. v. 63

I choose to see Him in my surroundings. They are filled with His _____. v. 64

We don't accept things as coincidence or random happenings. All is filtered through God's loving fingers and we acknowledge life as such.

❖ With what do you currently measure your life? Circle all that apply.

   job success, happy marriage, successful or well behaved children, health, wealth, power, possessions, famous people, friendships, intelligence, education

❖ Will you take all those circles to God, replacing them with His Word?

Friends of mine bought a brand new home with the inside still unfinished. They received a great price on it because of their willingness to finish it out themselves. For months they labored lovingly over their new home. This was where they would raise their children and create life long memories. All their hard work was evident in the final product – a breathtakingly beautiful house. In a short time, however, small cracks began to appear in the walls. In most situations minor settling and small cracking can be expected. In their case the cracks kept widening until they could slip their hands inside them and the house began tilting. They had done everything they knew to do and had contacted everyone they could think of for help. The bottom line was, their house had been built on a filled-in lake, a fact they had not been told. The fill was sinking and taking their house with it. Just as a faulty foundation can destroy a house, it can also destroy a life.

❖ Will you ask our loving, tender God to thoroughly examine your heart and mind?

❖ What is He revealing?

❖ What has the plumb line of God's Word shown you today?

Choose one of the six wise actions on pages 46 and 47. Write it below and commit, with God's help, to do it today.

Write the Life Lesson from Meditation 8 in your own words.

Video Experience Three

<u>On the Flip Side</u>

I. Life is _____.

II. Life requires _____.

III. Life involves _____.

49

Three godly outcomes of _____ .

a) It grows our _____ as we discover the
_____ of God.

b) It makes us _____ _____ _____.

c) It gives _____ to the _____.

"_____ is God's megaphone. There is no testimony without
a test. There is no message without a mess. There is no impact
without criticism."[6]

"Your greatest _____ will come out of
your_____ _____. We mistakenly think that the world
is impressed by how we handle prosperity, but the fact is the
world is impressed by how we handle adversity."[7]

*** When we are surrendered to Christ and live immersed in
His Word our lives always _____ _____ _____ ____
_____ _____ ____.

(videos are available for download at www.lynsmith.org)

Meditation 9: Read Psalm 119:65-72

Life Lesson - God, His Word, and His ways are good, and they are good for me all the time.

How can we gauge whether or not something is good when new studies constantly challenge that concept? Twenty-five years ago, pulsing the muscles during exercise was considered good for them. Now we stretch them out long and slow so we don't damage the joints, ligaments and tendons. Just a few years ago, all chocolate was fattening and was discouraged except in occasional and small doses. Now, dark chocolate is our friend (doing the happy dance). It lowers high blood pressure and contains heart healthy antioxidants which we are encouraged to take in every day. Eggs were bad. Now they can be good. New cars are touted as the best transportation available, until they are recalled due to faulty ignitions that burst into flame at random. The person we married promised to love us until death. Now they are with someone else and we are alone. The old good is tossed aside for the new good.

The writer of Psalm 119 makes an outrageous claim in verse 68. God is good and what He does is good. An absolute statement of truth. There is no exception clause. There are no specific circumstances that might exclude others. God *is* good and what He does *is* good. That does not mean life will always make sense to me, but it means I can trust the One who holds my life in His hand. It all makes perfect sense to Him. His ways are higher than mine so I yield my struggling mind to His incomparable intelligence and my limited body to His unmatched power. Because God is good and what He does is good, I can trust Him!

That does not mean I roll over and take a spiritual nap. Oh no! I pursue Him with everything in me. I love Him with all my heart, soul, mind and strength. He invites me to reason with Him (Isaiah 1:18 - *"Come now, let us reason together."*) and other Christ followers. Christianity is a thinking faith. It fully engages the mind. But in that engagement is an understanding of the vastness of God compared to my limitations. I joyfully respect who He is and who I am not … **God!**

❖ What two things do we pursue and ask God for, that help us understand His goodness? v. 68

❖ What is our primary source for knowing God? (hint – it is mentioned in almost every verse of Psalm 119)

A steady diet of secular television, movies, magazines, books, and the internet *will not* give us godly knowledge and good judgment. In fact, it will likely lead us away from those things, away from sound godly thinking.

Part of acquiring godly knowledge and good judgment is in reading what is good.

When our experiences don't seem good, when in fact we are in tremendous pain, we cling to the truth of God's goodness by flooding our minds with His Word. We ask God to teach us His knowledge and good judgment so we can accurately assess our situations and rightly respond. If we are filling our minds with a steady diet of secular information, we will process our lives through secular information, which is mainly godless and self-centered. That will *not* lead to good judgment but to a confusing mix of spiritual and pop psychology. Those belief systems will not withstand intense suffering, crushing pressure, or excruciating heartbreak.

❖ What word does the Psalmist use to describe his painful experience? vv. 67 and 71

❖ What positive word does he use to describe it? v. 71

❖ What were the results of his experience and discovery? vv. 67 and 71

Suffering makes us bitter or better. God allows suffering to draw us to Himself. Sometimes He allows what He hates to accomplish what He loves.[8] Our suffering is intended to take us to deep places with God – where we discover He is really there, He is really strong, He is really able and He is really enough! Suffering is part of the process of realizing God's goodness.

❖ What repeated phrase in verse 69 do we see for the fourth time? (vv. 10, 34, 58)

No matter who says what, I listen to God. I read His Word. I give Him all my attention so I can hear what He is saying, so I can then respond His way. All my heart is not 75%. It is not 99%. It is 100% God's! It is 100% trust. It is 100% His will. It is 100% devoted. That happens as I realize that everything about God is good … and good for me.

❖ How does the writer describe the heart of the arrogant? v. 70

The KJV says their heart is as fat as grease. The Hebrew word for fat means to be thick or, figuratively, to be stupid.[9] A thick heart cannot be penetrated but one which delights in God's Word softens. His truth can get through and be applied. A calloused, unfeeling heart is not wise. It is not taking in truth, is not delighting in God's goodness and is therefore making sinful, destructive choices.

❖ How does he describe his own heart in that same verse?

❖ Based on these descriptions, how would you describe your heart?

❖ To what does the Psalmist compare God's Word and with what result? v. 72

He discovered what Solomon knew years before when he chose knowledge and good judgment over wealth. Money can only buy so much. God, His Word and His ways are limitless!

When golf ball sized hail pummeled our windows, breaking through and causing an expensive mess, was God good? Every time our sweet Chihuahua had a seizure and I held his convulsing body, was God good? When my daughter was having a CAT scan to check for liver damage after a car accident, was God good? When my mother died of leukemia during the ninth month of my pregnancy, was God good? The resounding answer that echoes through the ages and bounces off every moment that ticks by is YES! That is why I can ponder those questions with a relaxed body and peaceful mind. My shoulders are not tense, my chest is not constricted, nor is my pulse racing. God is good all the time so I am at peace.

❖ Looking back, what deep disappointment, hurt or disillusionment have you experienced?

❖ What did you learn from it about God and about yourself?

❖ What recent disappointment or hurt have you experienced?

❖ What do you now know about God that enables you to respond differently this time?

❖ What current situation do you need to entrust to God's goodness?

Write the Life Lesson from Meditation 9 in your own words.

Meditation 10: Read Psalm 119:73-80

Life Lesson -Knowing God through His Word and intimate fellowship, enables me to share Him with others.

My mother was in full-time ministry. Many godly people came in and out of her life as well as our home. I have warm memories of listening to serious Bible learners and scholars discuss theology around the dining table. My sisters would scatter after the meal but I would stay and soak it all in. I loved it! There were a few people who stood out enough that I specifically remember them all these years later. They were so godly that, to my child eyes, they practically glowed. I would listen and stare enraptured. I wanted to hear more. I wanted to be like them.

In the years since, I have learned that glowing godliness comes only one way – through a consistent, intimate relationship with Jesus Christ.

❖ Read Exodus 34:4-8, 29, 33-35a. What happened to Moses from having been in God's presence?

❖ What began to happen over time and what did Moses do? 2 Corinthians 3:13

Like Moses, I have tried to fake God's radiance only to discover that insincerity breeds deep insecurity and self-consciousness. Whereas true intimacy with Christ breeds love, freedom and a refreshing lack of self-consciousness. Intimacy with Christ breeds God-consciousness. *He* radiates.

As we learn God's commands, put our hope in His Word, delight in His law, and meditate on His precepts, other Christ followers are drawn to us.

❖ Why do you think the writer connected our creation with God's Word? v. 73

❖ Read that verse again, but this time put "in order to" between the two phrases. What does that add to your understanding of the verse and our purpose?

❖ How does the Psalmist want other believers to respond to him? v. 74

The word rejoice in the original Hebrew means to be gleeful, glad, merry hearted and to cause to rejoice. What a significant effect to have on people! As we abide in Christ, others want to abide with us. His presence radiating from us draws them. But not just His presence.

❖ What quality has the Psalmist acquired by reading God's Word? v. 74

Our friends know when we read God's Word consistently because we always bring something fresh from Him to the conversation. We have hope for the hurting and the source of joy for the sad.

The writer challenges us again to associate suffering with deeper knowledge and understanding of God.

❖ What four things about God does he tell us we learn in suffering?

        God's _____. v. 75

        God's _____ _____. v. 76

        God's _____. v. 76

        God's _____. v. 77

A person who goes through that learning process multiple times comes out different, and it shows! Depth and maturity show.

❖ What does the Psalmist choose to do when he is mistreated? v. 78

❖ What is the result of this ongoing process in your life? v. 79

Other Christ followers come to expect wisdom from us as we meditate regularly on God's words. Although we cannot solve other people's problems, we can encourage, guide, strengthen, and comfort them from our storehouse of truth. As flawed as we are in ourselves, being earthen vessels or clay pots, the beauty, love and truth of Jesus Christ radiate through the cracks.

When He radiates out of us, we can relax and let Him shine. We don't have to *try* to shine or sparkle or glow. That's His job and He does it brilliantly! Our job is to stay at His feet, to bask in His presence, and to let Him fill us.

❖ How does 2 Corinthians 3:18 describe that process?

❖ Read Philippians 2:15-16. According to v. 15, whom are we to impact?

❖ According to v. 16, what are we to do?

"Go out into the world uncorrupted, a breath of fresh air in this squalid and polluted society. Provide people with a glimpse of good living and of the living God. Carry the light-giving Message into the night." Philippians 2:15-16 (The Message)

To put it simply, *GLOW*.

When I exalt Him, He draws people to Himself through His radiance in me. It is an awesome privilege to house the Spirit of the Living God.

❖ Who do you know that radiates Christ? What qualities do they have?

❖ How much time do you spend at the feet of Jesus? Talking to Him? Reading His Word?

❖ Can people come to you for fresh words from God? Do they?

❖ Would you say you are self-conscious or God-conscious? Whom do you think about the most?

Write the Life Lesson from Meditation 10 in your own words.

Meditation 11: Read Psalm 119:81-88

Life Lesson - When I am weak and weary God strengthens and sustains me through His word.

When was the last time you were truly tired? Not normal tired, not the-end-of-a-busy day tired, but bone tired. Weary to the core. The kind of tired that does not simply need a good night's sleep but needs a fresh infusion of strength and energy. We are not talking only about our bodies but our minds and hearts as well. There is a weariness that sets in when we have been in the battle a long time. From our passage today it sounds as though the Psalmist knew exactly what that feels like. It is comforting to know that thousands of years ago, people felt the same way we feel. They struggled with the same things we do and God's Word is still the answer. Praise!

Emotions:

❖ Which of the writer's expressions can you relate to in vv. 81-84?

❖ What words describe his soul? v. 81

The Psalmist is desperately longing for God's help. He didn't have the Holy Spirit's indwelling presence as we do today. He was yearning to experience God.

The Hebrew word for "faints" is *kalah* which means to perish, to consume away, to destroy utterly. [10] The Message uses the word "homesick."

❖ How would you describe what it feels like to long for someone or someplace?

❖ What word describes his eyes? v. 82

❖ For what is he longing? v. 82b

❖ On what does Hebrews 12:2 tell us to focus?

❖ Where does Psalm 121:1-2 tell us to look and what comes from there?

❖ As we look up, who is looking down? Psalm 121:5a

What an intimate connection is made when we lift our eyes!

❖ In verses 82 and 84, he uses the word 'when', which indicates he is waiting. Psalm 40:1 and 130:5-6 describe two different ways of waiting. What are they?

❖ What interesting illustration does he use to describe himself? v. 83

The Amplified version says, "blackened and shriveled." Wineskins exposed to soot and heat for a long time became discolored and parched. The integrity of the leather was compromised rendering them useless. They simply hung on the hook, empty, until the owner of the vineyard threw them away.

The Psalmist had waited so long for God to act that he felt parched and useless. Yet, he overcame his feelings with belief in God's Word. The Psalmist believed that God had not left him hanging but that He would rescue and restore him. He chose belief in what God said over his circumstances and how he felt.

Enemies:

❖ How does the Psalmist describe his enemies? vv. 84-85

Pitfalls are intended to throw us off track, trip us up, or injure us. They are dug with malicious intent, by devious people, who are acting against God's character and Word.

❖ How bad did it get? v. 87

❖ Did he deserve any of it? v. 86b

❖ What did he want God to do? v. 84b

He was having more than a bad day! It sounds like he had been hanging on for a long time and was exhausted.

Often in the midst of difficulty we wonder how long it will last. If we could just see the end date we could make it. If we knew how much more endurance it would take we could hang on. If we knew how much strength it would require we could keep going. Did the question in verse 84 sound familiar ... how long must I wait? That simple question can be full of emotion. What in the world is going on? Am I doing something wrong? God, what are you waiting for? What is the point here? Am I missing it? How long will this last?

❖ What does Hebrews 4:15 tell us and how does that comfort you?

❖ What does Hebrews 4:16 invite us to do and how does that encourage you?

In God's mercy He does not tell us how long our difficulties will last. He promises to be enough to get us through. He wants to teach us dependence on Him and He wants to show Himself strong on our behalf. The truth is, we can make it no matter how long it lasts because we are more than conquerors through Him who loves us (Romans 8:37).

Exclamation:

❖ How do we conquer through Him? vv. 87-88

We don't forget His words in the midst of the mess, we trust His commands because they never steer us wrong, we cling to His Word no matter how hard it gets, and we obey what He tells us. We may get weary, but God's Word always applies and is always relevant for every need.

❖ God supplies the power but I must participate by doing what? Isaiah 30:18-19

When we are getting weary, we need strong support. The best, unfailing, always available, Word of God is what we are to call upon. Relieve the pressure by claiming God's promises and putting your hope in what He says is true of you, true of Him and true of your situation. God's words are trustworthy. Take in large doses of them and be nourished, strengthened and renewed.

❖ What battle are you in right now? How long has it been going on?

❖ Describe your spiritual (and physical if it pertains) condition at this point in the battle.

❖ Will you memorize verse 81 to strengthen you in your battle? Write it in the space provided. Work on it until you can share it with someone or quote it in your group time.

❖ Will you faithfully take in His Word every day to remain supported?

If you are enjoying a season of relative calm, I encourage you to faithfully read God's Word every day in preparation for the next battle, and be available to someone who might need a little propping up from a friend.

❖ If you know someone in a battle, will you write down a few of our Psalm 119 verses and give them as encouragement? A woman who went through this Psalm 119 experience had a family member suffering a wrenching personal crisis. She was out of comforting words to say and had no more helpful advice to give. Knowing that God's Word was so much more powerful than anything she could offer, she wrote some of the Psalm 119 verses on note cards and slipped them into the family member's purse during lunch. Later that day, those verses provided the exact comfort needed to keep trusting, keep hoping and keep believing God.

Write the Life Lesson from Meditation 11 in your own words.

Meditation 12: Read Psalm 119:89-96

Life Lesson - God's Word is eternal and unfailing. It applies to every area of my life.

You have no doubt heard the expression: "Only two things in life are certain – death and taxes." Here's some good news! Even more certain than those two things are God and His Word. We can use those two things interchangeably since Christ is the living Word.

❖ How does John 1:1,14 explain that truth?

In the New Testament era of grace, we know that Jesus Christ is also the Word of God. The writer of Psalm 119 was specifically referring to the written Word, not yet knowing how it would be made flesh. But as we study, we can keep in mind that these truths and principles also apply to Jesus.

There are three themes in this section.

1) God's Word is Eternal.

❖ How does the Psalmist describe that quality? vv. 89, 90, 96

It is impossible to get our finite minds around the concept of eternity. We live in a time frame and our minds think in increments of time. That is one of the ways we live orderly lives. Think … how many clocks, watches, phones, and computers do you have that display the time? Write the number.
If you are like me, you are surprised by that number!

Therefore, it is hard for us to grasp a reality that exists outside of time: eternity. It goes back beyond the past and ahead beyond the future. It surrounds us in the present. Its vastness makes time seem small and temporary. That is the Biblical essence of time because one day time will cease and we will exist in eternity only. No more clocks. No more schedules. No more calendars. No time frame such as day and night. No time, but all the time we can imagine, so to speak.

We can understand time, so we tend to invest in the things that are time-sensitive, such as bank accounts, homes, education, careers, appearance, luxury, travel, and hobbies, to name a few. However, time-sensitive things will one day disappear and our lives will be evaluated by our relationship with God and our relationships with other people.

❖ How are we to love God and other people? Luke 10:27

Not only will things disappear but they disappoint. Bank accounts empty, homes burn, jobs are lost, looks fade, and possessions lose their luster.

❖ How does Isaiah compare the world with God's Word? Isaiah 40:8

It is time spent in God's Word, developing our intimacy with Christ, and impacting other people, that will become eternal treasures.

2) God's Word is Unfailing
The fact that God's Word is eternal implies that it never fails. How could it last that long if it had flaws that caused failure? Things that fail are cast aside for better models or for different concepts altogether. The Bible has not been cast aside because

it isn't flawed. There are individuals that choose to reject its truth but it remains the best seller of all time.

❖ Where else does the Bible stand firm? v. 89

❖ What word is used to describe God? v. 90

He is immutable = unchangeable, changeless. He is never out of date and never goes out of style. He isn't a trend and He isn't passé.

❖ How long do His laws endure? v. 91

God's words still make sense. They are still relevant. They are still perfect advice. They do not fail us … ever!

Because God's Word cannot and has not failed, it has been the foundation of millions, if not billions, of lives.

3) God's Word is Applicable

❖ How does the Psalmist feel about God's Word? v. 92a

❖ What would he have done without it? v. 92b

If we didn't have the truth and God's character, we would at least fail and probably give up in hard times. But we take in the powerful words of God and are helped, encouraged, and strengthened.

❖ What has God's Word done for him? vv. 93-94

❖ How does Hebrews 1:3 explain that further?

❖ When the writer is in trouble, what does he do? v. 95

❖ What else are we to do? 2 Corinthians 10:5

❖ According to verse 96, God's commands are what?

They don't run out. There is always something from God that we can cling to, that applies to our situation, that will give us wisdom, that will help us through, that will heal us, and that will give us joy

❖ List your treasures.

❖ Circle the ones that are eternal.

Ask God to help you emotionally surrender to Him your treasures that are not eternal. God does not forbid us to have earthly things but He does instruct us not to love them.

"*Do not love the world or anything in the world. If anyone loves the world, love for the Father is not in him.*" 1 John 2:15
A good way to evaluate your emotional investment in something is to ask yourself if you would be willing to let someone in need borrow it. If not, it likely has an emotional hold on you that is causing selfishness rather than fostering generosity.

❖ Where have you seen God's faithfulness in your life?

❖ Where do you need to see it now?

❖ What are you dealing with right now that needs a promise
  or an instruction from God?

❖ Look up verses that will help you in a concordance or
  online resource.

Write the Life Lesson from Meditation 12 in your own words.

Video Experience Four

The Goodness of God

_____ _____ _____, and _____ _____ _____ _____

_____. Psalm 119:68

I. God's _____

II. God's _____

III. Our _____

1) _____ _____

2) _____ _____ _____

*** God ____ _____ all the time, and His

_____ ____ _____ _____ every

_____ of every _____.

(videos are available for download at www.lynsmith.org)

Meditation 13: Read Psalm 119:97-104

Life Lesson - Consistently saturating my mind with God's Word changes me, enabling me to confidently make decisions that benefit my life and glorify God.

❖ What is the Psalmist's exclamation? v. 97

❖ What do you love about the Bible?

"Oh, how I love all You've revealed." Psalm 119:97 (The Message)

It is God's gift to us, His personal decision to reveal Himself. That isn't only worth our attention, but our life commitment!

❖ How does the writer express his commitment to God's Word? v. 97

When we love God's Word, we cannot get it off our minds. Some of it is conscious choice as we discipline our minds to memorize The Word and apply it. Some is just because we love it! It becomes part of us and permeates all we do.

Meditating on it "all day long" implies we either wake up with it on our minds from the night before or we start our day with it.

❖ Does the Bible stay fresh on your mind best when you read it at night before you go to bed or first thing in the morning before starting your day?

Three things God's Word does for our minds:

1) It makes us _____. v. 98

"*They give me an edge on my enemies.*" (The Message)
Wise means having the power of discerning and judging properly as to what is true or right[11]
Wisdom is the ability to make good use of knowledge[12]

Wisdom isn't just being smart, not just knowing a lot, and not just being well educated.

Read 1 Kings 3:16-28
God gave Solomon the ability to take situational information and make the best decision with it. God does the same thing for us through the reading of His Word. Daily intake of it enables us to take daily events and make right decisions about them. It is a supernatural process that takes place in our minds as we immerse ourselves in God's character, thoughts, and ways. They begin to become ours.

2) It gives us _____. v. 99

God's Word enables us to read between the lines, to see and hear what isn't obvious.
Insight means an instance of apprehending the true nature of a thing, especially through intuitive understanding, penetrating mental vision or discernment; faculty of seeing into inner character or underlying truth.[13]
We know it is important to be good listeners, but listening doesn't always help unless we can hear what is not being said. The ability to discern what is behind words is God-given, and is often in proportion to both time spent in His Word and the amount of control we yield to the Holy Spirit within us.

Immersion in God's Word also gives us the capability to discern truth in the midst of deception and untruth, in a way that will help a person or situation. Our spiritual growth is *never* intended for someone's harm; rather for their ultimate good. When God gives us insight into someone's life it is *not* for the purpose of humiliating them but with the goal of helping them, whether through prayer, words or action.

❖ What insight did Jesus have in Luke 18:18-23?

❖ Who does the Psalmist have more insight than? v. 99

We don't have to be intimidated by someone's knowledge, because godly insight is much more valuable and powerful. It is supernatural!

3) It gives us _____. v. 100

Understanding is defined as a mental process of a person who comprehends; superior power of discernment; and enlightened intelligence.[14]

Filling our minds with God's Word actually does make us smarter! It is a combination of brain exercise as we read and memorize, and supernatural intervention.
God's Word does not return void. It goes in, it goes out, and it has power! It changes us. It literally changes our brains, thinking processes, connections, and perceptions.

❖ Who does the Psalmist have more understanding than? v. 100

While age has its advantages in experience, it does not always translate into having more understanding – *that* comes through a steady diet of God's Word. Don't let being younger than someone intimidate you. Always be respectful, but if an older person is not absorbing God's truth on a regular basis and you are, you will come out with more understanding of life than they.

❖ What two words describe God's plan for our minds? Romans 12:2

Intentionally, He does not say heart but mind. The mind is the thing that needs constant input of truth in order for us to *think* God's way about life, make right decisions, help people with their decisions, and discern situations.

When we begin to see our responses to things change, our thoughts becoming clearer and more resolved, and a more sensitive awareness of the Holy Spirit's promptings, then we experience what he describes in verse 103.

❖ Write verse 103 in your own words.

❖ What else, compared to God's Word, comes up short? Psalm 19:10
Nothing is better. *Nothing* else satisfies.

❖ When we make our decisions based on the wisdom, insight and understanding of God's Word, what do we hate and keep our feet from? vv. 101 and 104

When people say the Bible cannot answer all of life's questions because it does not contain certain subjects or that times have changed, they are totally missing the spiritual component of what constant saturation with God's Word does to our minds. It enables us to think and reason with God's thoughts and reasoning.

❖ List current situations where you need wisdom, insight and/or understanding.

❖ What does James 1:5 tell us to do and what will happen as a result?

For the remainder of our time in Psalm 119:

❖ Will you commit to ask God every day for wisdom in your specific situation?

❖ Will you commit to spend some time each day filling your mind with His Word?

❖ Will you commit to write down your thoughts every day as you read and talk with God about your situation?
What is sometimes sweeter to you than His Words or Himself?

Will you surrender those things to God and ask Him to develop in you a stronger craving for His Words and Himself?

Most of the time are you saturated or dry?

If you often feel dry spiritually, think about how much time you spend reading your Bible and talking to God. Are you willing to make those things more of a priority in your life?

Write the Life Lesson from Meditation 13 in your own words.

Meditation 14: Read Psalm 119:105-112

Life Lesson - The Bible is my lifelong guide for daily living.

Many summers my family drove out to the country to a fruit farm where we picked blackberries. Most of the way we traveled on smooth, paved streets. The last few miles, however, were on washboarded, dirt roads. The ruts were deep, with lots of rocks, and the Oklahoma dust was red and cloying.

The journey of life takes us over various surfaces. The Psalmist refers to that journey as our path. In this section, we want to look closely at several facets of the path.

1) The lamp

The lamp used was a small, bowl-like object containing oil and a wick for providing light.

❖ What did the lamp specifically illuminate? v. 105

At night, a lamp or light was held low so the walker could see to take steps. There was no other light than perhaps moon and stars. If there was significant cloud cover, it was extremely dark. The lamp would make a small circle of light around and in front of the walker's feet. It revealed just enough at a time to take the next step or two. There were no paved streets, although some were made of rough stone. People walked primarily on dirt roads and trails. Only the small area of path in front of them was illuminated.

Spiritually and figuratively:
the lamp = prosperity and/or instruction.[15]
light = enlightenment, happiness, and cheerfulness.[16]

God's Word is successful instruction to my feet and cheerfulness for my path.

❖ What does that mean for daily life?

Letting a lamp guide us involves trust. Since it only lights up a small space at a time, we can't see everything around us. We don't know the reasons, motives, reactions, or the big picture. We simply trust that when we take a step, God is in control of all those things.

We are all on a path that is uniquely ours. No one else will live our life. Only God knows how to walk it the best way, so *He* should be our source of guidance. We hold the lamp (the Word) and He illuminates the path. We move forward and He takes care of everything around us. If we could grasp and do just *that* on a regular basis, our lives would be radically transformed!

2) The Commitment

"I've committed myself and I'll never turn back from living by Your righteous order." v. 106 (The Message)

❖ What did Jesus say to the person who hesitates to go forward? Luke 9:61-62

❖ What happened to Lot's wife when she looked back at her former home? Genesis 19:26

God calls us forward. The light illuminates the path in front of us. Behind us is the old life, the old city, the old desires, and the old activities. The reason we are not to look back is so we won't be tempted to go back. Our eyes look ahead. Our feet move forward.

"Without focus, not only do obstacles overwhelm us, but we also become distracted and diffused by opportunities."[17]

It goes back to trusting God with what is around us, both good and bad. Opportunities sound good, but if they are not on the path God has for us, they are distractions.

❖ What has the Psalmist experienced a lot of? v. 107

Every path walked for and with God involves pain. Life in general involves pain, but the path of Christ certainly does - He promised that.

"For my determined purpose is that I may know Him, that I may progressively become more deeply and intimately acquainted with Him, perceiving and recognizing and understanding the wonders of His Person more strongly and more clearly, and that I may in that same way come to know the power outflowing from His resurrection which it exerts over believers, and <u>that I may so share His sufferings as to be continually transformed</u> in spirit into His likeness even to His death." Philippians 3:10 (Amplified)

Two things that cause suffering are: being like Christ, because the world won't like us; and being conformed into the image of Christ. He suffered, so we must also, to be like Him.

The Psalmist is saying that even if it is painful, we choose to follow the narrowly lighted path, taking each step, while trusting God completely.

3) The Passion

❖ How does the writer express himself to God? v. 108

The KJV says, "freewill offerings" which means plenty, spontaneously, voluntarily, and freely.

As a natural part of an intimate, dynamic spiritual journey, we will be filled with praise!

The more we discover God in His Word, the more He will pour forth from us. It sounds like a back and forth conversation throughout the day. He is on our minds and we see Him revealed, so our awareness of Him is heightened. We become God-sensitive. Interestingly, the Psalmist wrote that sentence right after having said he suffers much – *but* he praises willingly, freely, and spontaneously.

❖ What did two men do in a dire and painful situation? Acts 16:22-25

That kind of response is how we know our relationship with God is truly intimate, active, and vibrant.

❖ Though we face daily dangers, what keeps us strong and courageous? vv. 109, 110

4) The Inheritance

"Your statutes are my _____ _____." v. 111

The word "heritage" in Hebrew means to seize, to take into possession, to take or have for one's own, to possess for oneself

God's statutes become mine. They are not something only promised or that I'm waiting for but *mine*. God gave us instructions for the path that are perfect and personal. They belong to me!

❖ What did they become to the Psalmist, that can also be true for us? v. 111

The Message says, *"What a gift!"*

God didn't have to give the gift of His Word. He put two people here with whom He had perfect communion. *They* damaged that relationship, so God went to great lengths to fellowship with us and make Himself known in other ways – through prophets, the written Word, and Jesus. He didn't want to leave us here wandering aimlessly but showed us *the* path and gave us instructions for success. That *is* a gift! We are empowered on *this* path. *His* path!

5) The End

❖ On what did the Psalmist set his heart? v. 112
There is no retirement from loving and serving God. It is nowhere in the Bible. Those that loved God followed Him to the end of life.

❖ How old was Moses when he climbed the mountain to die alone with God? Deuteronomy 34:7

❖ Jacob was 147 years old when we see this precious picture of him. What did he do after he and Joseph finished talking? Genesis 47:31

Faithfulness to the end is only possible by staying close to the Lord; by not letting disappointment, bitterness, and fatigue take root.

❖ What are we to do with those kinds of defeating thoughts? 2 Corinthians 10:5b

"I concentrate on doing exactly what You say – I always have and always will." Psalm 119:112 (The Message)

Life is a long haul. It takes planning, training and intent to live it well.

❖ What does your path look like right now? Smooth, rutted, forked, filled with holes, covered with debris, or strewn with pebbles?

❖ How faithful are you in holding the lamp? How frequent is your Bible study time? How often do you seek God's guidance?

❖ How committed are you to God's path, no matter what it involves?

❖ How spontaneous is your praise? Is it scheduled at certain times or does it flow freely?

❖ What does that indicate about the intimacy you have with God?

Psalm 119:112 says, "*I concentrate on doing exactly what you say --- I always have and always will.*" *(The Message)*

How much of that statement is true of you - not from a legalistic Pass/Fail sense but as <u>the desire of your heart</u>?

Circle the number that most accurately describes you.
        1 = the least, 10 = the most

"I concentrate on doing exactly what You say"

                1 2 3 4 5 6 7 8 9 10

"I always have"   1 2 3 4 5 6 7 8 9 10

"I always will"   1 2 3 4 5 6 7 8 9 10

Write the Life Lesson from Meditation 14 in your own words.

Meditation 15: Read Psalm 119:113-120

Life Lesson - The more I read God's Word, the more I know and love Him, the more I love and read His Word. (this is an ongoing circular process)

❖ What people or things in your life do you appreciate or desire more the longer you have them?

Some things easily lose value over time and are discarded, while some grow more precious. In this section, the Psalmist contrasts the people and activities of the world to his awe and love of God's Word.

1) The Religious Undecided – vv. 113-114

"I hate the thoughts of undecided (in religion), double-minded people." Psalm 119:113 (Amplified)

There are those who approach religion like a buffet. They take a little bit of everything. Some claim Christianity but only accept the parts they like. Others who claim Christianity in all facets don't live it.

❖ In contrast, how does the writer feel? v. 113

In The Message, verse 113 reads, *"I love Your clear-cut revelation."*

God's Word is honest. We can trust it and God. It is straightforward, cutting through to the heart.

❖ How does Hebrews 4:12 describe that process?

God is not trying to trick us. We are not being mocked. He and His Word are the real deal! We won't find out He lied to us nor will we be ashamed at the end.

❖ How is God described? v. 114

The Message says, "*You're my place of quiet retreat.*"
He is our protection from confusion. He is the place we can withdraw to for reflection and clarity. His Word renews us when we have been confronted by puzzling people. We hope in Him. He is the only thing we can truly count on to be absolutely genuine every moment of every day.

2) Evildoers – v. 115

❖ Why does the Psalmist tell them to go away?

Some people are bad influences on us. It is hard to obey God, to hear His voice when sin is tugging at us. Some people are extremely persuasive, either by personality or emotional connection.

❖ How does 1 Corinthians 15:33 state that truth?

If one person standing up on a chair holds the hand of a similar sized person standing down on the floor, and they both pull, which one will win? The one on the floor will almost always pull the one on the chair down. It rarely goes the other way.

If we truly desire to obey God then we *will* end harmful relationships. We *will* wisely limit dangerous influence and only accept what we can handle without sinning.
We know where we are vulnerable. Cut off the temptation!

3) Disappointment – vv. 116-117

❖ Why does our hope in God not disappoint? Romans 5:5

We have all we need in the Person of the Holy Spirit. He comes through in the clutch. He is a Power Player. He thrives under pressure. When we put all our eggs in His basket, we win.

The world will disappoint us. People we love will disappoint us. We will disappoint ourselves. God will *never* disappoint! He may be slow in our timing, He may be mysterious in some situations but ultimately He will never disappoint.

"We find ourselves standing where we always hoped we might stand – out in the wide open spaces of God's grace and glory, standing tall and shouting our praise." Romans 5:5 (The Message)

What a beautiful picture and expression of our response to His faithfulness! When we risk all without a safety net, He shows up and we are changed.

❖ Not only will we not be disappointed, but what else is promised? Romans 9:33, 10:11

4) The Rebellious – vv. 118-119

❖ What does God do to those who refuse His Word? vv. 118, 119

Their choices lead to death. Their flippant attitudes toward God and casual sin are their ultimate destruction. Drunkenness, drug use, sex outside marriage – things in our entertainment that make us laugh are tragic in real life.

Why do we laugh at the things for which Jesus died, and for which many people will spend eternity separated from God?

❖ What is the writer's response? v. 119

The Message says, "*I lovingly embrace everything You say*." I will not rebel against even the smallest instruction or encouragement. I will *love* God's Words, God's help for me, and God's boundaries for me.

5) Our Response – v. 120

❖ What does it mean for a child of God to tremble in fear of Him?

❖ Do you think awe is different? If so, how?

Recognition of God leads to worship. Acknowledging His power, holiness, justice, sovereignty, and majesty should take us to our knees. We are amazed we have been spared! We are stunned that God loves us, wants us, delights in us, and sings over us.

Our response is total devotion.

❖ What events or people has God used to turn you to Him?

❖ What difficulty or disappointment are you struggling in or with now?

❖ What can you choose to believe about it and about God?

❖ What qualities is God building in you through your current situation?

❖ How will you express your awe of God?

Write the Life Lesson from Meditation 15 in your own words.

Meditation 16: Read Psalm 119:121-128

Life Lesson - A personal relationship with God enables me to claim His promises and trust His actions.

❖ Think about a very personal relationship you have or have had. What qualities or vivid memories stand out?

In this section of Psalm 119, the writer describes his personal relationship with God and how he benefits from it.

I. The Psalmist's Relationship with God

A. Purpose

V. 121 – "I have done what is _____ and _____." The Hebrew word for "just" is *tsedeq:* the right thing whether nationally, morally or legally. In an ethical sense, it is what ought to be.[18]

❖ What is causing the writer's concern? v. 121

God calls us to be faithful to Him in every situation. We are to do what is morally, legally, and ethically right – to follow God's high standard.

B. Position

❖ What word does the writer use to describe himself? vv. 122, 124, 125

❖ Describe the relationship between an owner and his/her servant.

❖ What are the expectations of each?

❖ What happened to a servant who chose to stay with his master? Deuteronomy 15:12-17

❖ In light of that, what does Psalm 40:6 mean to you?

Read Psalm 123:2. "Servants of Bible times were trained to anticipate the needs of their masters. Over many years they became so sensitive to what their masters wanted that they would not have to be told or commanded. A glance or a hand gesture would be enough to send them into action."[19]

C. Pursuit

❖ What action is the Psalmist taking? v. 123

❖ How do these verses express the same concept? Psalm 25:15, 105:4, 119:2, 58; Hebrews 12:1-2a

❖ How do you do that in your life?

D. Passion

❖ How does the writer feel about God's commands? v. 127

❖ How does David feel about God's Word? Psalm 19:7-10

- ❖ How did these two men feel about the Scriptures? Luke 24:32

- ❖ How does Paul exhort us about The Word? Colossians 3:16a

- ❖ Considering these descriptions, would you say you are passionate about God's Word?

E. Purity

- ❖ What does the Psalmist consider all of God's precepts to be? v. 128

- ❖ What is the result? v. 128

Saturating my mind with God's Word causes me to love it and hate sin.

- ❖ What are we told about evil versus good? Romans 12:9, Isaiah 5:20

- ❖ What did David learn about sin? Psalm 32:3-5, 51:3-4

II. The Benefits to the Psalmist of his Relationship with God

A. Protection

"Do not _____ me." v. 121

"_____ your servant's well-being." v. 122

❖ What does God promise us? Hebrews 13:5

❖ What is the name of the Lord and what does He promise us? Proverbs 18:10

B. Promises

"My eyes fail, looking for Your _____." v. 123

❖ How does Jesus describe our salvation? John 10:28

"Deal with Your servant according to Your _____." v. 124

❖ With what does God crown us? Psalm 103:4

❖ How long does God's love last? Psalm 89:28

"Give me _____ that I may _____."
v. 125

❖ What are we promised? James 1:5

C. Power

❖ What does the Psalmist want God to do? v. 126

❖ What do we learn about God? Psalm 89:13

❖ What kind of action can God take? Psalm 18:13-15

❖ What three things does God use on our behalf and why? Psalm 44:3b

❖ Looking back at the five areas of intimacy with God (purpose, position, pursuit, passion, purity), describe your personal intimacy with Him.

❖ In which areas do you need to be more intimate with God and how can you do that?

❖ What promise has God brought to mind that you need to claim for yourself or for someone in your life?

❖ What action is God taking in your life that you need to trust?

❖ What actions do you want Him to take that require your trust?

Write the Life Lesson from Meditation 16 in your own words.

Meditation 17: Read Psalm 119:129-136

Life Lesson - God enables Christ followers to understand and obey His Word.

"Your statutes are _____; therefore I _____ them." v. 129

❖ Write the command from each of these passages and explain how obeying it is wonderful.

      Luke 9:23

      Ephesians 4:32

      Ephesians 4:29

We studied "lamp" and "light" in v. 105, but here we see a different word associated with light.

"The _____ of Your words gives light." v. 130

"Unfold" means to spread or open out, lay open to view, to reveal or display, to become clear, apparent, or known.[20]

❖ How would you apply that definition to God's Word and light?

Unfolding is a process. We can't read God's Word in one sitting and be done for life. We can't get it all in a month, a year, or five years. It must be continuously unfolded one piece at a time, each piece revealing more of the whole of God.

❖ How does it give understanding to the simple? John 16:13, 15

❖ When someone says they cannot understand the Bible, is that true? Why or why not?

❖ Write verse 131 in your own words. Is that description true of you?

❖ Who is guaranteed God's mercy? v. 132b

❖ When do they have it? v. 132b

❖ Is there ever a moment when we are not loved, wanted, and cared for?

❖ When it feels like we are not loved, wanted, or cared for, who or what is the problem?

"Let no _____ _____ over me." v. 133

❖ How do we do that? 119:11

❖ What else can we do to protect ourselves from sin? Ephesians 6:13

- ❖ From what does the Psalmist ask to be redeemed and why? v. 134

- ❖ How does oppression make it difficult to obey God?

- ❖ What does the Psalmist ask God to do for him? v. 135a

- ❖ How does Numbers 6:25-26 describe that?

- ❖ Who did Jesus look at that way? Write the phrase from Mark 10:21

- ❖ Do you think He also looked at Peter that way? Why or why not? Luke 22:61, Romans 2:4

- ❖ How does the writer respond to the disobedience of God's law? v. 136

- ❖ When was the last time you cried over sin - yours or someone else's?

Crying over the consequences of sin isn't the same thing as crying over the sin itself. If we truly understand what sin does to people and the high price Jesus had to pay for it, we will hate it and grieve over it.

- ❖ What do you understand better after studying vv. 129-136?

❖ Is there an obedient action you need to take?

Write the Life Lesson from Meditation 17 in your own words.

Video Experience Five

<u>The Process of Change</u>

I. _____ through _____ and _____

II. _____ _____ _____

III. _____ _____ _____

IV. _____, _____ and

_____ new _____

*** _____ and _____

_____ come through allowing God's Word to

_____ us and His Holy Spirit to _____ us.

(videos are available for download at www.lynsmith.org)

Meditation 18: Read Psalm 119:137-144

Life Lesson - We can always count on God and His Word because they are always right.

❖ Briefly describe a time when God did or allowed something in your life that you resisted, thought was not right, or prayed against.

❖ Briefly describe something going on right now that you resent, wish was different, don't understand, or are praying against.

1) God is always right.

❖ List the verses in this section that contain the words "right", "righteous" or "righteousness".

The Hebrew word for righteous is *tsaddlyq:* just, in the sense of a just forensic (used in courts of law or public discussion or debate) cause.[21]

God is lawful, honest, and right. He is the standard of ethics and morality. He is the just Judge. He makes the right decisions.

Just is not the same as fair. God is not fair, He is just. Justice means doing what is right. Fair means making everything equal. God does not treat us all equally. His blessings look different from person to person. He disciples us according to our personalities, our actions and what He knows we need. He is specific and personal. He is just, not fair.

Because He and His words are always right and fully trustworthy, we don't have to question them. We can always ask what He wants us to learn and apply. But we don't need to ask Him to explain Himself so we can accept what is said or what is happening.

His actions of justice and righteousness reflect His just and right character.

❖ What qualities of God do you like, and tend to emphasize?

❖ Which ones do you not like, and try to ignore?

❖ How are the ones you don't like, actually beneficial?

2) His Word can be tested.

❖ The Psalmist thoroughly tested God's promises. What was the result? v. 140

❖ Why would he feel that way after testing the promises?

❖ What promise, verse or knowledge of God have you clung to through a difficulty?

❖ How has God fulfilled a promise in your life?

3) His Word becomes my delight.

❖ Why is the writer worn out? v. 139

When we live out our journey with Jesus passionately, we are going to encounter people who mock us, work against us, pressure us and lie to us. They don't listen to the truth.

❖ How does Paul encourage us? Galatians 6:9

❖ How does the writer describe himself? v. 141

Our situations or what people say about us can distort in our minds the truth of who we are. Like the writer, we need to remember what *God* says.

❖ How does God refer to us in Deuteronomy 32:10?

❖ How does God love us? Jeremiah 31:3

❖ What two words describe His love for us? Isaiah 43:4

❖ What has God done with us? Isaiah 49:16

❖ Which of those verses is the most comforting to you and why?

❖ What is the Psalmist experiencing? 119:143a

❖ What delights him in the middle of it? v. 143b

Go back and look at what you wrote down at the beginning of Meditation 18.

❖ Is what God is doing or allowing in your life, right for you? How do you know?

❖ What about God are you testing through this?

❖ What truth from this Meditation will you apply and choose to delight in, in your situation?

Write the Life Lesson from Meditation 18 in your own words.

Meditation 19: Read Psalm 119:145-152

Life Lesson - When I cry out to God according to His Word, He hears and answers.

❖ What recent answer to prayer have you seen?

❖ How much of the Psalmist's heart is engaged in calling out to the Lord? v. 145

❖ What has he committed to do when he gets the answer? v. 145

❖ Is that your commitment when you pray, no matter what the answer is?

What we see in the Psalmist isn't a half-hearted, mediocre attempt. He isn't hurrying through a prayer time.

This is a whole-hearted effort. A calling out from the depths of his being. He is calling out with his heart – not just with his mind, voice, or body, but his heart! The heart is the seat of our emotions and passions.

❖ What do you think is the significance in his choice of the word *heart*?

❖ What is the Psalmist's simple prayer in verse 146?

When we don't know what else to pray, simple words can be the very best. Our words don't have to be complicated. We say what we can and trust God to know what we really need.

❖ Who helps us pray? Hebrews 7:25, Romans 8:26

❖ When does the writer pray? v. 147

❖ What does that indicate about him?

Our life choices reflect how much we think we need God. What we are willing to give up for God's power and closeness in our lives reveals the true condition of our hearts.

❖ What is your first priority every day?

❖ When does the Psalmist meditate on God's promises? v. 148

❖ When are we to meditate on God's Word? Psalm 1:2

❖ How does that challenge you?

❖ Through what filter does the Psalmist ask God to hear him? v. 149

❖ According to verse 150, who is near him?

❖ Who else is near? v. 151

❖ How is that similar to what we read in 2 Kings 6:8-17?

"_____ _____ I learned from Your statutes" v. 152

The writer had a relationship with God that had been tested and proven. He *knew* God. The longer we know Him, the more we see of His faithfulness, and the deeper we trust Him.

❖ How long will God's Word last? v. 152

❖ How many other things will last that long?

❖ How can that knowledge help you prioritize your passions and your time?

In vv. 145-148, we see the words – *obey, keep, put my hope in, meditate on* – referring to the writer's approach to God's Word. As he is calling out and crying out to God, he stays in His Word. The guaranteed way to know that you are praying according to God's heart and will, is to pray His own words back to Him.

❖ What situation do you need to cry out to God about? Not necessarily take action, just pour your heart out in accordance with His Word?

Read vv. 145-152 out loud, this time as a prayer. It is already written in first person so, as you read it, use those personal pronouns as honestly coming from you. This is praying Scripture back to God.
❖ Do you believe He hears and answers?

❖ What are you willing to give up to make Him the priority of your life?

Write the Life Lesson from Meditation 19 in your own words.

Meditation 20: Read Psalm 119:153-160

Life Lesson - Because God's Word is true and eternal, I can trust and obey it without fear.

1) The Psalmist's problems

"Look upon my _____" v. 153

"_____ my _____" v. 154

"Salvation is far from the _____" v. 155

"Many are the _____ who _____ me" v. 157

"I look on the _____" v. 158

Verse 158 in The Message says – "*I took one look at the quitters and was filled with loathing; they walked away from Your promises so casually!*"

Even other Hebrews were deserting him, did not trust, and did not believe.

What a warning for us to not take God's promises casually! Learn them and claim them. They are God's gifts to us. He makes Himself available to us, so don't quit when it's hard.

❖ What are your current challenges?

2) The Psalmist's prayer

"_____ me" v. 153

"_____ me" v. 154

"_____ my life" vv. 154, 156, 159

That phrase is used three times but in three different ways.

"according to Your _____" v. 154

He is claiming what God said. He is believing it is true and it is for him.

"according to Your _____" v. 156

He is claiming God's justice, to do what is right.

"according to Your _____" v. 159

He is claiming God's compassion toward him in his hardships.

3) The Psalmist's platform

He knew God, so he knew how and what to pray.

"I have not _____ Your law" v. 153

"I have not _____ from Your statutes" v. 157

"I _____ Your precepts" v. 159

4) The Psalmist's proclamation

❖ What does he say about God's words? v. 160

There are absolutes. What God says doesn't waver or change. Some of His truths can be applied in different ways, but the foundational fact is that He is the Author of what is true because He *is* Truth. We can resist it and Him, but only to our detriment.

❖ What two words describe God's Word? v. 160b

When the writer's mess is resolved, when kingdoms rise and fall, when the earth is no more, *God's Word* will remain. Backing up and seeing what we can of the big picture of God, helps us properly respond to our individual situations. It helps us understand that what we are experiencing has a bigger purpose than just us. Therefore, we can trust the One who knows the entire plan and can handle all the things we cannot.

❖ Write Isaiah 26:3

❖ How confidently do you take God's Word to Him and pray it?

❖ Is there a situation for which you are afraid to pray God's will because you think you won't like it?

❖ What is there to fear in God's will?

❖ If you believe these things, how will it change your prayer time and Bible reading this week?

Write the Life Lesson from Meditation 20 in your own words.

Meditation 21: Read Psalm 119:161–168

Life Lesson - Obedience to God's Word brings joy and peace.

1) Joy

❖ What reaction does the writer have to God's Word?
    v. 161

The KJV says, "standeth in awe." The Hebrew word is *pachad* which means to be startled, to be afraid, to palpitate with joy, to make to tremble.[22] Obviously, the writer experiences strong physical and emotional reactions or responses to what he reads.

❖ What responses have you had to God's Word during your study of Psalm 119?

❖ What is the writer's response in verse 162a?

❖ To what does he compare it? v. 162b

That term refers to all the possessions left by a conquered people, such as homes, money, costly jars, jewelry, clothing and livestock. Incredible wealth!

God's Word is breathtaking. Imagine being shown an estate decorated exactly in your tastes, with multiple garages filled with your favorite cars, a state-of-the-art gym, a luxurious theater room, acres of prize-winning horses, a tennis court, an olympic-sized swimming pool with waterfalls, a full staff, all the money needed for upkeep, and being handed the deed of ownership. How would you feel?

Does God's Word make you feel like that?

❖ What is the contrast in verse 163?

❖ In your own words, describe how it feels to be lied to versus how it feels to be told the truth.

❖ What is your response to the fact that God always tells you the truth?

❖ For what does the Psalmist praise God, and how often? v. 164

Seven is the perfect number in the Bible. This verse simply means we praise God many times a day as a natural outflow of time spent reading His Word, and of the intimacy that develops as a result.

❖ Why does the writer obey God's Word? v. 167

This is obedience with joy! It isn't done grudgingly, sadly or with questions. It is done with ultimate worry-free trust that produces joy.

❖ What else do we learn about joy?

    Nehemiah 8:10

    Psalm 16:11

Psalm 51:12

Psalm 97:11

James 1:2

2) Peace

❖ Who has peace? v. 165

❖ What benefit do they enjoy? v. 165

The KJV says, "nothing shall offend them." The Hebrew word for offend is *mikshol* which means stumbling block, an obstacle, a cause of falling or sinning, an enticement (especially an idol)[23]

❖ Explain that benefit in your own words.

❖ What two things does the writer do? v. 166

Sometimes we need to wait for God to reveal something, but even in the waiting, we are to remain faithful to what He has already shown us. Godly waiting is not passive but rather purposefully calm and expectant. It requires deep trust without fear and impatience.

❖ What is known to God? v. 168

Peace comes when we understand that we are thoroughly known and absolutely loved. Peace thrives where there are no secrets, only healthy and honest exposure. Rather than being a scary thing, being known by God is safe. His love for us overcomes anything sinful or unpleasant about us. God is the best one to open ourselves up to because His responses will always be right and filled with love.

Secrets are a prison. Transparency is freedom.

❖ What else do we learn about peace?

Psalm 34:14

Proverbs 14:30

Isaiah 9:6

Isaiah 26:3

Isaiah 32:17

John 16:33 and Ephesians 2:14

Romans 5:1

Write the Life Lesson from Meditation 21 in your own words.

Meditation 22: Read Psalm 119:169-176

Life Lesson - A life of praise comes from a life immersed in God's Word.

"May my _____ come before You, O Lord" v. 169

"May my _____ come before You" v. 170

"May my _____ overflow with _____" v. 171

"May my _____ _____ of Your Word" v. 172

"Let me live that I may _____ You" v. 175

All of those expressions are connected with God's Word.

Praise (v. 171) in Hebrew is *T'hillah* meaning a hymn, a song of praise which exults in God.[24]

Exult means to show or feel a lively or triumphant joy; rejoice exceedingly; be highly elated or jubilant.[25]

❖ The Psalmist is specifically praising God for teaching him His decrees. Thinking about the definition of "exult", use your own words to describe how he feels.

People who don't praise are not reading and applying God's Word regularly.

Two things happen when we consistently read and apply:

1) Intimacy with God deepens. Our relationship with Him becomes satisfying. He becomes our Best Friend, Partner, Someone to talk to, Someone who listens, Someone who cares and Someone who acts on our behalf. We are not alone. We know Someone intimately and He knows us!

2) His Words guide, help us make decisions, give us clarity, answer questions, make us wise, free us from fear, and give us security.

Praising, thinking of God, and talking to God become second nature. It happens as part of the process the Psalmist introduced in 119:1-2.

❖ What does the writer confess? v. 176

The Hebrew word is *taah* which means to vacillate or to stray, to err, to wander.

❖ What does he ask God to do for him? v. 176

❖ What does God do for us? John 10:3, Luke 15:1-6

Write the Life Lesson from Meditation 22 in your own words.

Closing

These last two sections paint a compelling, dynamic picture of a Christ follower whose life is filled with joy, peace, and praise.

Jesus said we are not to look like the world. We are to be different. If we have joy, peace and praise in our lives we *will be* different.

❖ Do these three qualities describe you? If not, why not, and what needs to happen in your life to cultivate these qualities?

❖ Describe the difference between the Holy Spirit-grown qualities of joy, peace and praise, and …

Forced enthusiasm:

Rose-colored glasses:

What do you praise God for from your study of Psalm 119?

Video Experience Six

<u>What Matters Most</u>

"God created us for this: to live our lives in a way that makes him look more like the _____ and the _____ and the _____ _____ that He really is. This is what it means to be created in the image of God."[26] (John Piper)

Our lives are meant to be magnificent _____ ____ _____, which means we don't just _____ but we _____!

I. God's Word is to be the _____ of my

_____.

II. God's Word is to be the _____of my

_____.

***What matters most in life is _____ to God

and _____ _____ with everything in me.

(videos are available for download at www.lynsmith.org)

Endnotes

[1] *Life Application Bible*, New International Version. (Wheaton: Tyndale House Publishers, Inc., 1991), 1036.

[2] Dictionary.com, http://www.dictionary.reference.com/browse/revival?s=t (accessed 1 June 2010).

[3] James Strong. Strong's Exhaustive Concordance of the Bible. (Nashville: Broadman & Holman Publishing, 1999), #2421.

[4] Chip Ingram, *Living on the Edge*. (New York: Howard Books, 2009), 223.

[5] Strong, #5769.

[6] Adelle M. Banks, *Rick Warren to Pastors: 'There is no testimony without a test'* http://www.religionnews.com/2014/06/09/rick-warren-pastors-testimony-without-test/ (accessed 28 June 2014).

[7] Ibid.

[8] Joni Eareckson Tada, *Quotes*. https://www.goodreads.com/quotes/12065-sometimes-god-allows-what-he-hates-to-accomplish-what-he (accessed 20 August 2014).

[9] Bible Hub, http://biblehub.com/lexicon/psalms/119-70.htm. (accessed 10 June 2010).

[10] Strong, #3615.

[11] Dictionary.com, http://www.dictionary.reference.com/browse/wise?s=t (accessed 15 June 2010).

[12] Dictionary.com, http://www.dictionary.reference.com/browse/wisdom?s=t (accessed 15 June 2010).

[13] Dictionary.com, http://dictionary.reference.com/browse/insight?s=t. (accessed 16 June 2010)

[14] Dictionary.com,
http://www.dictionary.reference.com/browse/understanding?s=t (accessed 17 June 2010).

[15] Spiros Zodhiates, ed. Hebrew-Greek Key Word Study Bible. (Chattanooga: AMG Publishers, 1996), 1614.

[16] Zodhiates, 1576.

[17] Erwin McManus, *Wide Awake.* (Nashville: Thomas Nelson, 2008), 136.

[18] Zodhiates, 1630.

[19] George W. Knight, *The Illustrated Guide to Bible Customs and Curiosities.* (Uhrichsville, Ohio: Barbour Publishing, Inc., 2007), 124.

[20] Dictionary.com,
http://www.dictionary.reference.com/browse/unfolding?s=t (accessed 29 June 2010).

[21] Zodhiates, 1630.

[22] Zodhiates, 1627.

[23] Zodhiates, 1606.

[24] Zodhiates, 1652.

[25] Dictionary.com, http://dictionary.reference.com/browse/exult?s=t. (accessed 9 July 2010).

[26] John Piper, *Quotes.*
https://www.goodreads.com/author/quotes/25423.John_Piper (accessed 19 July 2014).

Journeying friend ...

How I would love to hear about your Psalm 119 experience!

I hope you joined our Facebook community where lovers of God's Word are encouraging one another on their journey through *WORD*. It's a place where we are sharing Scripture, God stories, and hope. If you haven't yet, you may join us at *The Psalm 119 Experience*.

If you prefer to interact with me in other social media ways, visit www.lynsmith.org where you will find all my connecting information. I look forward to hearing from you!

If you would like me to share with your group God's amazing rescue of my life from the pit of sexual abuse and destruction, please send an email to connect@lynsmith.org.

All other speaking requests can also be sent to connect@lynsmith.org.

That God would use a formerly broken person to shine the Light of hope and wholeness into others is humbling in ways that take me to my knees daily. It is there that I surrender myself to Jesus for His purposes. If His purposes and your needs align, then please know I am at your service.

Journeying with you,

Lyn

Made in the USA
Columbia, SC
27 August 2019